ENCOURAGE-
MENT
for
MOTHERS

Words of Confidence and Hope

compiled by Michelle L. Geiman

Dear Tara,
    Remember God holds
motherhood in the highest
regard.   Love Mom

Harold Shaw Publishers
Wheaton, Illinois

CONTENTS

Grateful acknowledgment is made to the publishers of the Scripture versions, portions of which are quoted in this book, using the following abbreviations:

JB	The Jerusalem Bible
KJV	The King James Version
NASB	The New American Standard Bible
NIV	The New International Version
NKJV	The New King James Version
PHILLIPS	The New Testament in Modern English by J. B. Phillips
RSV	The Revised Standard Version
TEV	Today's English Version
TLB	The Living Bible

Portions from:

The Jerusalem Bible, copyright © 1966 by Darton, Longman & Todd, Ltd. and Doubleday, a division of Bantam Doubleday Dell Publishing Group, Inc. Reprinted by permission.

The *New American Standard Bible,* © 1960, 1962, 1963, 1968, 1971, 1972, 1973, 1975, 1977 by The Lockman Foundation. Used by permission.

The *Holy Bible: New International Version,* Copyright © 1973, 1978, 1984 International Bible Society. Used by permission of Zondervan Publishing House. All rights reserved.

The New King James Version. Copyright © 1979, 1980, 1982, Thomas Nelson Inc., Publishers.

The *New Testament in Modern English,* Revised Edition by J. B. Phillips, © J. B. Phillips, 1958, 1960, 1972.

The Revised Standard Version of the Bible, Copyright 1946, 1952, 1971 by the Division of Christian Education of the National Council of the Churches of Christ in the USA, and used by permission.

Today's English Version (The Good News Bible), © American Bible Society, 1976. Used by permission.

The Living Bible, © 1971. Used by permission of Tyndale House Publishers, Inc., Wheaton, IL 60189. All rights reserved.

RELYING ON GOD'S PROVISION

"Lord
I crawled
across the barrenness
to you
with my empty cup
uncertain
in asking
any small drop
of refreshment.
If only
I had known you
better
I'd have come
running
with a bucket."
Nancy Spielberg

Our fathers trusted in You; they trusted, and You delivered them.
Psalm 22:4, NKJV

The righteous call to the LORD, and he listens; he rescues them from all their troubles.
Psalm 34:17, TEV

Take delight in the LORD, and he will give you the desires of your heart.
Psalm 37:4, RSV

In all my years I have never seen the Lord forsake a man who loves him; nor have I seen the children of the godly go hungry.
Psalm 37:25, TLB

Cast your burden upon the LORD, and He will sustain you; He will never allow the righteous to be shaken.
Psalm 55:22, NASB

Only test me! Open your mouth wide and see if I won't fill it. You will receive every blessing you can use!
Psalm 81:10, TLB

The LORD will protect you from all evil; He will keep your soul. The LORD will guard your going out and your coming in from this time forth and forever.
Psalm 121:7-8, NASB

The eyes of all look expectantly to You, and You give them their food in due season. You open Your hand and satisfy the desire of every living thing.
Psalm 145:15-16, NKJV

The God who made both earth and heaven, the seas and everything in them . . . is the God who keeps every promise.
Psalm 146:6, TLB

The blessing of the LORD brings wealth,
and he adds no trouble to it.
Proverbs 10:22, NIV

Trust in your money and down you
go! Trust in God and flourish as a tree!
Proverbs 11:28, TLB

For the Lord is faithful to his promises. Blessed are all those who wait for
him to help them.
Isaiah 30:18, TLB

I give water in the wilderness, rivers
in the desert, to give drink to my chosen people, the people whom I
formed for myself that they might
declare my praise.
Isaiah 43:20-21, RSV

Even before they finish praying to me,
I will answer their prayers.
Isaiah 65:24, TEV

"I am the LORD, the God of all mankind. Is anything too hard for me?"
Jeremiah 32:27, NIV

The LORD is good, a refuge in times of trouble. He cares for those who trust in him.
Nahum 1:7, NIV

For this reason I say to you, do not be anxious for your life, as to what you shall eat, or what you shall drink; nor for your body, as to what you shall put on. But seek first His kingdom and His righteousness; and all these things shall be added to you. Therefore do not be anxious for tomorrow; for tomorrow will care for itself. Each day has enough trouble of its own.
Matthew 6:25, 33-34, NASB

Therefore I say to you, all things for which you pray and ask, believe that

you have received them, and they shall be granted you. And whenever you stand praying, forgive, if you have anything against anyone; so that your Father also who is in heaven may forgive you your transgressions.
Mark 11:24-25, NASB

Do not be anxious about your life, what you shall eat, nor about your body, what you shall put on. For life is more than food, and the body more than clothing.
Luke 12:22-23, RSV

All mankind scratches for its daily bread, but your heavenly Father knows your needs. He will always give you all you need from day to day if you will make the Kingdom of God your primary concern.
Luke 12:30-31, TLB

Don't worry about anything; instead, pray about everything; tell God your needs, and don't forget to thank him for his answers.
Philippians 4:6, TLB

Just as you trusted Christ to save you, trust him, too, for each day's problems; live in vital union with him.
Colossians 2:6, TLB

Keep your lives free from the love of money and be content with what you have, because God has said, "Never will I leave you; never will I forsake you."
Hebrews 13:5, NIV

For the Lord is watching his children, listening to their prayers.
1 Peter 3:12, TLB

As you know him better, he will give you, through his great power, everything you need for living a truly good life: he even shares his own glory and his own goodness with us!
2 Peter 1:3, TLB

This is the confidence that we have in him, that, if we ask any thing according to his will, he heareth us: And if we know that he hear us, whatsoever we ask, we know that we have the petitions that we desired of him.
1 John 5:14-15, KJV

WHEN I FEEL ALONE

"The soul hardly ever realizes it, but whether he is a believer or not, his loneliness is really a homesickness for God."
Hubert Van Zeller

Have I not commanded you? Be strong and courageous! Do not tremble or be dismayed, for the LORD your God is with you wherever you go.
Joshua 1:9, NASB

In the morning, O LORD, you hear my voice; in the morning I lay my requests before you and wait in expectation.
Psalm 5:3, NIV

The friendship of the LORD is for those who fear him, and he makes known to them his covenant.
Psalm 25:14, RSV

The LORD Almighty is with us; the God of Jacob is our fortress.
Psalm 46:7, NIV

I will remember the works of the LORD: surely I will remember thy wonders of

old. I will meditate also of all thy work, and talk of thy doings.
Psalm 77:11-12, KJV

If I take the wings of the morning and dwell in the uttermost parts of the sea, even there thy hand shall lead me, and thy right hand shall hold me.
Psalm 139:9-10, RSV

"You will seek me and find me when you seek me with all your heart. I will be found by you," declares the LORD.
Jeremiah 29:13-14, NIV

And be sure of this—that I am with you always, even to the end of the world.
Matthew 28:20, TLB

I will not leave you as orphans; I will come to you.
John 14:18, NASB

Neither height nor depth, nor anything else in all creation, will be able to separate us from the love of God that is in Christ Jesus our Lord.
Romans 8:39, NIV

Let each of you look not only to his own interests, but also to the interests of others.
Philippians 2:4, RSV

Come close to God and he will come close to you.
James 4:8, PHILLIPS

GOD'S LOVING GUIDANCE

"The voice of the subconscious argues with you, tries to convince you; but the inner voice of God does not argue, does not try to convince you. It just speaks and is self-authenticating."
E. Stanley Jones

I will teach you what you are to do.
Exodus 4:15, NASB

He guides the humble in what is right
and teaches them his way.
Psalm 25:9, NIV

I will instruct you and teach you in the
way you should go; I will counsel you
and watch over you.
Psalm 32:8, NIV

For such is God, our God forever and
ever; He will guide us until death.
Psalm 48:14, NASB

You guide me with your counsel, and
afterward you will take me into glory.
Psalm 73:24, NIV

Praise the Lord! For all who fear God
and trust in him are blessed beyond

expression. Yes, happy is the man who delights in doing his commands.
Psalm 112:1, TLB

Thy word is a lamp to my feet and a light to my path. The unfolding of thy words gives light; it imparts understanding to the simple.
Psalm 119:105, 130, RSV

You chart the path ahead of me and tell me where to stop and rest. Every moment you know where I am. You both precede and follow me and place your hand of blessing on my head.
Psalm 139:3, 5, TLB

For the LORD gives wisdom, and from his mouth come knowledge and understanding.
Proverbs 2:6, NIV

In all your ways acknowledge him, and he will make your paths straight.
Proverbs 3:6, NIV

Whether you turn to the right or to the left, your ears will hear a voice behind you, saying, "This is the way; walk in it."
Isaiah 30:21, NIV

And I will lead the blind by a way they do not know, in paths they do not know I will guide them. I will make darkness into light before them and rugged places into plains.
Isaiah 42:16, NASB

This plan of mine is not what you would work out, neither are my thoughts the same as yours! For just as the heavens are higher than the earth, so are my ways higher than yours, and my thoughts than yours.
Isaiah 55:8-9, TLB

The LORD will guide you continually, and satisfy your desire with good things.
Isaiah 58:11, RSV

Then I will give you shepherds after my own heart, who will lead you with knowledge and understanding.
Jeremiah 3:15, NIV

O Lord, I know it is not within the power of man to map his life and plan his course—so you correct me, Lord.
Jeremiah 10:23-24, TLB

Jesus replied, "If anyone loves me, he will obey my teaching. My Father will love him, and we will come to him and make our home with him."
John 14:23, NIV

He has made known to us in all wisdom and insight the mystery of his

will, according to his purpose which
he set forth in Christ.
Ephesians 1:9, RSV

If you want to know what God wants
you to do, ask him, and he will gladly
tell you, for he is always ready to give
a bountiful supply of wisdom to all
who ask him.
James 1:5, TLB

GOD-GIVEN SELF-WORTH

"God carries your picture in his wallet."
Tony Campolo

"God does not love us because we are valuable. We are valuable because God loves us."
Archbishop Fulton J. Sheen

"God hugs you."
Saint Hildegarde of Bingen

He found him in a desert land, and in
the howling waste of the wilderness;
he encircled him, he cared for him, he
kept him as the apple of his eye.
Deuteronomy 32:10, RSV

The LORD seeth not as man seeth; for
man looketh on the outward appear-
ance, but the LORD looketh on the
heart.
1 Samuel 16:7, KJV

Behold, Thou dost desire truth in the
innermost being, and in the hidden part
Thou wilt make me know wisdom.
Psalm 51:6, NASB

For you created my inmost being; you
knit me together in my mother's
womb. I praise you because I am fear-
fully and wonderfully made; your
works are wonderful, I know that full
well. My frame was not hidden from

you when I was made in the secret place. When I was woven together in the depths of the earth, your eyes saw my unformed body. All the days ordained for me were written in your book before one of them came to be.
Psalm 139:13-16, NIV

He has made everything beautiful in its time.
Ecclesiastes 3:11, RSV

Fear not, for I have redeemed you; I have summoned you by name; you are mine.
Isaiah 43:1, NIV

I will be your God through all your lifetime, yes, even when your hair is white with age. I made you and I will care for you. I will carry you along and be your Savior.
Isaiah 46:4, TLB

He will hold you aloft in his hands for all to see—a splendid crown for the King of kings. Never again shall you be called "The God-forsaken Land" or the "Land That God Forgot." Your new name will be "The Land of God's Delight" and "The Bride," for the Lord delights in you and will claim you as his own.

Isaiah 62:3-4, TLB

I have loved you with an everlasting love; therefore I have drawn you with lovingkindness.

Jeremiah 31:3, NASB

But even the very hairs of your head are all numbered. Fear not therefore: ye are of more value than many sparrows.

Luke 12:7, KJV

You did not choose Me, but I chose you and appointed you that you should go and bear fruit, and that your fruit should remain, that whatever you ask the Father in My name He may give you.

John 15:16, NKJV

We are able to hold our heads high no matter what happens and know that all is well, for we know how dearly God loves us, and we feel this warm love everywhere within us because God has given us the Holy Spirit to fill our hearts with his love.

Romans 5:5, TLB

For his Holy Spirit speaks to us deep in our hearts and tells us that we really are God's children.

Romans 8:16, TLB

Do you not know that you are God's temple and that God's Spirit dwells in you?
1 Corinthians 3:16, RSV

Or do you not know that your body is a temple of the Holy Spirit who is in you, whom you have from God, and that you are not your own? For you have been bought with a price: therefore glorify God in your body.
1 Corinthians 6:19-20, NASB

And God is able to make all grace abound to you, so that in all things at all times, having all that you need, you will abound in every good work.
2 Corinthians 9:8, NIV

We who believe are carefully joined together with Christ as parts of a beautiful, constantly growing temple for God.

And you also are joined with him and with each other by the Spirit and are part of this dwelling place of God.
Ephesians 2:21-22, TLB

For God did not give us a spirit of timidity, but a spirit of power, of love and of self-discipline.
2 Timothy 1:7, NIV

What is man, that thou art mindful of him? or the son of man, that thou visitest him? Thou madest him a little lower than the angels; thou crownedst him with glory and honour, and didst set him over the works of thy hands.
Hebrews 2:6-7, KJV

Your beauty should not come from outward adornment, such as braided hair and the wearing of gold jewelry and fine clothes. Instead, it should be

that of your inner self, the unfading beauty of a gentle and quiet spirit, which is of great worth in God's sight.
1 Peter 3:3-4, NIV

This is how we know what love is: Jesus Christ laid down his life for us.
1 John 3:16, NIV

VALUING OUR CHILDREN

"Children will invariably talk, eat, walk, think, respond, and act like their parents. Give them a goal to work toward. Give them a pattern that they can see clearly, and you give them something that gold and silver cannot buy."
Billy Graham

Only be careful, and watch yourselves closely so that you do not forget the things your eyes have seen or let them slip from your heart as long as you live. Teach them to your children and to their children after them.

Deuteronomy 4:9, NIV

Keep his decrees and commands . . . so that it may go well with you and your children after you and that you may live long in the land the LORD your God gives you for all time.

Deuteronomy 4:40, NIV

And these words, which I command thee this day, shall be in thine heart: And thou shalt teach them diligently unto thy children, and shalt talk of them when thou sittest in thine house, and when thou walkest by the way, and when thou liest down, and when thou risest up.

Deuteronomy 6:6-7, KJV

We will not hide them from their children; we will tell the next generation the praiseworthy deeds of the LORD, his power, and the wonders he has done.
Psalm 78:4, NIV

For he established a testimony in Jacob, and appointed a law in Israel, which he commanded our fathers, that they should make them known to their children: That the generation to come might know them ... That they might set their hope in God, and not forget the works of God, but keep his commandments.
Psalm 78:5-7, KJV

May the LORD make you increase, both you and your children. May you be blessed by the LORD, the Maker of heaven and earth.
Psalm 115:14-15 NIV

Sons are a heritage from the LORD, children a reward from him. Like arrows in the hands of a warrior are sons born in one's youth. Blessed is the man whose quiver is full of them.
Psalm 127:3-5, NIV

He who spares the rod hates his son, but he who loves him is careful to discipline him.
Proverbs 13:24, NIV

He who fears the LORD has a secure fortress, and for his children it will be a refuge.
Proverbs 14:26, NIV

Children's children are the crown of old men; and the glory of children are their fathers.
Proverbs 17:6, KJV

The just man walketh in his integrity: his children are blessed after him.
Proverbs 20:7, KJV

Train a child in the way he should go, and when he is old he will not turn from it.
Proverbs 22:6, NIV

The rod and reproof give wisdom, but a child who gets his own way brings shame to his mother. Correct your son, and he will give you comfort; he will also delight your soul.
Proverbs 29:15, 17, NASB

Therefore, whoever humbles himself like this child is the greatest in the kingdom of heaven. See that you do not look down on one of these little ones. For I tell you that their angels in

heaven always see the face of my Father in heaven.
Matthew 18:4, 10, NIV

Do not provoke your children to anger; but bring them up in the discipline and instruction of the Lord.
Ephesians 6:4, NASB

Do not exasperate your children, that they may not lose heart.
Colossians 3:21, NASB

By this we know that we love the children of God, when we love God and observe His commandments.
1 John 5:2, NASB

GOD AS PARENT

"Can't you see the Creator of the universe, who understands every secret, every mystery . . . sitting patiently and listening to a four-year-old talk to him? That's a beautiful image of a father."
James C. Dobson

God created man in his own image, in the image of God created he him; male and female created he them.
Genesis 1:27, KJV

He is the LORD; let him do what is good in his eyes.
1 Samuel 3:18, NIV

Though my father and mother forsake me, the LORD will receive me.
Psalm 27:10, NIV

The counsel of the LORD standeth for ever, the thoughts of his heart to all generations.
Psalm 33:11, KJV

He is like a father to us, tender and sympathetic to those who reverence him.
Psalm 103:13, TLB

You are precious to me and honored, and I love you.
Isaiah 43:4, TLB

O LORD, you are our Father. We are the clay, you are the potter; we are all the work of your hand.
Isaiah 64:8, NIV

As a mother comforts her child, so will I comfort you.
Isaiah 66:13, NIV

I will heal their waywardness and love them freely, for my anger has turned away from them.
Hosea 14:4, NIV

To all who received him, who believed in his name, he gave power to become children of God.
John 1:12, RSV

My sheep hear my voice, and I know them, and they follow me; and I give them eternal life, and they shall never perish, and no one shall snatch them out of my hand.
John 10:27, RSV

Blessed be the God and Father of our Lord Jesus Christ, a gentle Father and the God of all consolation, who comforts us in all our sorrows, so that we can offer others, in their sorrows, the consolation that we have received from God ourselves.
2 Corinthians 1:3-4, JB

I will be a Father to you, and you will be my sons and daughters, says the Lord Almighty.
2 Corinthians 6:18, NIV

For now we are all children of God through faith in Jesus Christ.
Galatians 3:26, TLB

Through God you are no longer a slave but a son, and if a son then an heir.
Galatians 4:7, RSV

My son, do not make light of the Lord's discipline, and do not lose heart when he rebukes you, because the Lord disciplines those he loves, and he punishes everyone he accepts as a son.
Hebrews 12:5-6, NIV

Endure hardship as discipline; God is treating you as sons. For what son is not disciplined by his father?
Hebrews 12:7, NIV

He is patient with you, not wanting
anyone to perish, but everyone to come
to repentance.
2 Peter 3:9, NIV

Behold, what manner of love the
Father hath bestowed upon us, that
we should be called the sons of God.
1 John 3:1, KJV

CELEBRATING LIFE'S GOODNESS

"With the goodness of God to desire our highest welfare, the wisdom of God to plan it, and the power of God to achieve it, what do we lack?"
A. W. Tozer

You . . . shall rejoice in all the good things the LORD your God has given to you and your household.
Deuteronomy 26:11, NIV

Yours, O LORD, is the greatness and the power and the glory and the majesty and the splendor, for everything in heaven and earth is yours. Yours, O LORD, is the kingdom; you are exalted as head over all. Wealth and honor come from you; you are the ruler of all things. In your hands are strength and power to exalt and give strength to all.
1 Chronicles 29:11-12, NIV

But let all those rejoice who put their trust in You; let them ever shout for joy, because You defend them; let those also who love Your name be joyful in You.
Psalm 5:11, NKJV

Therefore my heart is glad and my tongue rejoices; my body also will rest secure.
Psalm 16:9, NIV

Thou dost show me the path of life; in thy presence there is fulness of joy, in thy right hand are pleasures for evermore.
Psalm 16:11, RSV

Trust in the LORD, and do good; dwell in the land and cultivate faithfulness.
Psalm 37:3, NASB

Praise the LORD, O my soul; all my inmost being, praise his holy name. Praise the LORD, O my soul, and forget not all his benefits—who forgives all your sins and heals all your diseases, who redeems your life from the pit and crowns you with love and compassion, who satisfies your desires

with good things so that your youth is renewed like the eagle's.
Psalm 103:1-5, NIV

It is the living who give thanks to Thee, as I do today; a father tells his sons about Thy faithfulness.
Isaiah 38:19, NASB

Burst into songs of joy together, you ruins of Jerusalem, for the LORD has comforted his people, he has redeemed Jerusalem.
Isaiah 52:9, NIV

For you shall go out with joy, and be led out with peace; the mountains and the hills shall break forth into singing before you, and all the trees of the field shall clap their hands.
Isaiah 55:12, NKJV

I will greatly rejoice in the LORD, my soul shall be joyful in my God; for he hath clothed me with the garments of salvation, he hath covered me with the robe of righteousness, as a bridegroom decketh himself with ornaments, and as a bride adorneth herself with her jewels.
Isaiah 61:10, KJV

My people shall be satisfied with my goodness, says the LORD.
Jeremiah 31:14, RSV

I will rejoice in the LORD, I will joy in the God of my salvation.
Habakkuk 3:18, KJV

Now unto him that is able to keep you from falling, and to present you faultless before the presence of his glory with exceeding joy, to the only wise God our Saviour, be glory and majesty, dominion and power, both now and ever. Amen.

Jude 24-25, KJV

LIVING OUT GOD'S PURPOSES

"To accept the will of God never leads to the miserable feeling that it is useless to strive anymore. God does not ask for the dull, weak, sleepy acquiescence of indolence. He asks for something vivid and strong. He asks us to cooperate with him, actively willing what he wills, our only aim, his glory."
Amy Carmichael

This book of the law shall not depart out of your mouth, but you shall meditate on it day and night, that you may be careful to do according to all that is written in it; for then you shall make your way prosperous, and then you shall have good success.
Joshua 1:8, RSV

Commit everything you do to the Lord. Trust him to help you do it, and he will.
Psalm 37:5, TLB

How can a young man keep his way pure? By guarding it according to thy word. With my whole heart I seek thee; let me not wander from thy commandments!
Psalm 119:9-10, RSV

Our mouths were filled with laughter, our tongues with songs of joy. Then it was said among the nations, "The LORD

has done great things for them." The
LORD has done great things for us, and
we are filled with joy.
Psalm 126:2-3, NIV

Honor the LORD from your wealth,
and from the first of all your produce;
so your barns will be filled with
plenty, and your vats will overflow
with new wine.
Proverbs 3:9-10, NASB

Commit to the LORD whatever you do,
and your plans will succeed.
Proverbs 16:3, NIV

He who guards his mouth and his
tongue guards, his soul from troubles.
Proverbs 21:23, NASB

The man who works hard sleeps well.
Ecclesiastes 5:12, TLB

Whatever your hand finds to do, do it
with all your might, for in the grave,
where you are going, there is neither
working nor planning nor knowledge
nor wisdom.
Ecclesiastes 9:10, NIV

Learn to do right! Seek justice, encourage the oppressed. Defend the
cause of the fatherless, plead the case
of the widow.
Isaiah 1:17, NIV

I don't want your sacrifices—I want
your love; I don't want your offer-
ings—I want you to know me.
Hosea 6:6, TLB

What does the LORD require of you
but to do justice, and to love kindness, and to walk humbly with your
God?
Micah 6:8, RSV

If you love me, you will keep my commandments.
John 14:15, RSV

My command is this: Love each other
as I have loved you.
John 15:12, NIV

And do not be conformed to this world,
but be transformed by the renewing
of your mind, that you may prove what
the will of God is, that which is good
and acceptable and perfect.
Romans 12:2, NASB

Do not be deceived: "Bad company
corrupts good morals."
1 Corinthians 15:33, NASB

For freedom Christ has set us free;
stand fast therefore, and do not sub-
mit again to a yoke of slavery.
Galatians 5:1, RSV

If we live by the Spirit, let us also walk by the Spirit. Let us not become boastful, challenging one another, envying one another.
Galatians 5:25-26, NASB

Share each other's troubles and problems, and so obey our Lord's command.
Galatians 6:2, TLB

And let us not grow weary in well-doing, for in due season we shall reap, if we do not lose heart.
Galatians 6:9, RSV

It is God himself who has made us what we are and given us new lives from Christ Jesus; and long ages ago he planned that we should spend these lives in helping others.
Ephesians 2:10, TLB

Be humble and gentle. Be patient with each other, making allowance for each other's faults because of your love. Try always to be led along together by the Holy Spirit and so be at peace with one another.

Ephesians 4:2-3, TLB

Let no unwholesome word proceed from your mouth, but only such a word as is good for edification according to the need of the moment, that it may give grace to those who hear.

Ephesians 4:29, NASB

Let all bitterness, and wrath, and anger, and clamour, and evil speaking, be put away from you, with all malice: And be ye kind one to another, tenderhearted, forgiving one another, even as God for Christ's sake hath forgiven you.

Ephesians 4:31-32, KJV

Live a life worthy of the Lord and . . .
please him in every way: bearing fruit
in every good work, growing in the
knowledge of God, being strength-
ened with all power according to his
glorious might so that you may have
great endurance and patience, and
joyfully giving thanks to the Father,
who has qualified you to share in the
inheritance of the saints in the kingdom of light.
Colossians 1:10-12, NIV

Let your roots grow down into him
and draw up nourishment from him.
See that you go on growing in the
Lord, and become strong and vigor-
ous in the truth you were taught. Let
your lives overflow with joy and
thanksgiving for all he has done.
Colossians 2:7, TLB

Set your minds on things above, not on earthly things.
Colossians 3:2, NIV

Put on then, as God's chosen ones, holy and beloved, compassion, kindness, lowliness, meekness, and patience, forbearing one another and, if one has a complaint against another, forgiving each other; as the Lord has forgiven you, so you also must forgive. And above all these put on love, which binds everything together in perfect harmony.
Colossians 3:12-14, RSV

And whatever you do or say, let it be as a representative of the Lord Jesus, and come with him into the presence of God the Father to give him your thanks.
Colossians 3:17, TLB

Obey your earthly masters in every-thing; and do it, not only when their eye is on you and to win their favor, but with sincerity of heart and rever-ence for the Lord.
Colossians 3:22, NIV

Whatever you do, work at it with all your heart, as working for the Lord, not for men, since you know that you will receive an inheritance from the Lord as a reward. It is the Lord Christ you are serving.
Colossians 3:23-24, NIV

Now we exhort you, brethren, warn those who are unruly, comfort the faint-hearted, uphold the weak, be pa-tient with all.
1 Thessalonians 5:14, NKJV

You are God's man. Run from all these evil things, and work instead at what

is right and good, learning to trust
him and love others and to be patient
and gentle.
1 Timothy 6:11, TLB

The whole Bible was given to us by
inspiration from God and is useful to
teach us what is true and to make us
realize what is wrong in our lives; it
straightens us out and helps us do
what is right. It is God's way of making us well prepared at every point,
fully equipped to do good to everyone.
2 Timothy 3:16-17, TLB

Because he himself suffered when he
was tempted, he is able to help those
who are being tempted.
Hebrews 2:18, NIV

But encourage one another daily, as
long as it is called Today, so that none

of you may be hardened by sin's deceitfulness.
Hebrews 3:13, NIV

Try to stay out of all quarrels, and seek to live a clean and holy life, for one who is not holy will not see the Lord.
Hebrews 12:14, TLB

It is God's will that your good lives should silence those who foolishly condemn the Gospel without knowing what it can do for them, having never experienced its power. You are free from the law, but that doesn't mean you are free to do wrong. Live as those who are free to do only God's will at all times. Show respect for everyone.
1 Peter 2:15-17, TLB

Quietly trust yourself to Christ your Lord, and if anybody asks why you believe as you do, be ready to tell him,

and do it in a gentle and respectful way.
1 Peter 3:15, TLB

Learn to put aside your own desires so that you will become patient and godly, gladly letting God have his way with you.
2 Peter 1:6, TLB

It is a loyal thing you do when you render any service to the brethren, especially to strangers.
3 John 5, RSV

WORDS OF COMFORT
AND ENCOURAGEMENT

"You don't have to be alone in your hurt! Comfort is yours. Joy is an option. And it's all been made possible by your Savior. He went without comfort so that you might have it. He postponed joy so that you might share in it. He willingly chose isolation so that you might never be alone in your hurt and sorrow."
Joni Eareckson Tada

And He said, "My Presence will go with you, and I will give you rest."
Exodus 33:14, NKJV

The LORD your God is he that goeth with you, to fight for you against your enemies, to save you.
Deuteronomy 20:4, KJV

The Lord is still in his holy temple; he still rules from heaven. He closely watches everything that happens here on earth.
Psalm 11:4, TLB

Weeping may go on all night, but in the morning there is joy.
Psalm 30:5, TLB

You have rescued me, O God who keeps his promises. I worship only you.
Psalm 31:6, TLB

The LORD is near to the brokenhearted, and saves those who are crushed in spirit.
Psalm 34:18, NASB

The good man does not escape all troubles—he has them too. But the Lord helps him in each and every one.
Psalm 34:19, TLB

O Lord my God, many and many a time you have done great miracles for us, and we are ever in your thoughts.
Psalm 40:5, TLB

For the Lord is always good. He is always loving and kind, and his faithfulness goes on and on to each succeeding generation.
Psalm 100:5, TLB

For His lovingkindness is great toward us, and the truth of the LORD is everlasting.
Psalm 117:2, NASB

This is my comfort in my affliction, for Your word has given me life.
Psalm 119:50, NKJV

Those who love your laws have great peace of heart and mind and do not stumble.
Psalm 119:165, TLB

Those who trust in the LORD are like Mount Zion, which cannot be shaken but endures forever. As the mountains surround Jerusalem, so the LORD surrounds his people both now and forevermore.
Psalm 125:1-2, NIV

Those who sow in tears will reap with songs of joy. He who goes out weeping, carrying seed to sow, will return with songs of joy, carrying sheaves with him.

Psalm 126:5-6, NIV

When my spirit grows faint within me, it is you who know my way.

Psalm 142:3, NIV

The Lord is just in all his ways, and kind in all his doings. The Lord is near to all who call upon him, to all who call upon him in truth.

Psalm 145:17-18, RSV

Great is our Lord and mighty in power; his understanding has no limit.

Psalm 147:5, NIV

The LORD takes pleasure in those who fear Him, in those who hope in His mercy.
Psalm 147:11, NKJV

The name of the LORD is a strong tower; the righteous run to it and are safe.
Proverbs 18:10, NIV

The victory belongs to the LORD.
Proverbs 21:31, RSV

He gives power to the faint, and to him who has no might he increases strength.
Isaiah 40:29, RSV

But they that wait upon the LORD shall renew their strength; they shall mount up with wings as eagles; they shall

run, and not be weary; and they shall walk, and not faint.
Isaiah 40:31, KJV

Do not fear, for I am with you; do not anxiously look about you, for I am your God. I will strengthen you, surely I will help you, surely I will uphold you with My righteous right hand.
Isaiah 41:10, NASB

I, the LORD, have called you in righteousness; I will take hold of your hand. I will keep you.
Isaiah 42:6, NIV

The LORD will comfort Zion; he will comfort all her waste places, and will make her wilderness like Eden, her desert like the garden of the LORD; joy and gladness will be found in her, thanksgiving and the voice of song.
Isaiah 51:3, RSV

I, even I, am he that comforteth you.
Isaiah 51:12, KJV

The mountains shall depart, and the hills be removed; but my kindness shall not depart from thee, neither shall the covenant of my peace be removed, saith the LORD that hath mercy on thee.
Isaiah 54:10, KJV

"I will restore you to health and I will heal you of your wounds," declares the LORD.
Jeremiah 30:17, NASB

I will forgive their wickedness and will remember their sins no more.
Jeremiah 31:34, NIV

Come, let us return to the LORD; for he has torn, that he may heal us; he has stricken, and he will bind us up.
Hosea 6:1, RSV

For you who fear my name the sun of righteousness shall rise, with healing in its wings.
Malachi 4:2, RSV

Come to me, all you who are weary and burdened, and I will give you rest. Take my yoke upon you and learn from me, for I am gentle and humble in heart, and you will find rest for your souls. For my yoke is easy and my burden is light.
Matthew 11:28-30, NIV

With men this is impossible; but with God all things are possible.
Matthew 19:26, KJV

I am leaving you with a gift—peace of mind and heart! And the peace I give isn't fragile like the peace the world gives. So don't be troubled or afraid.
John 14:27, TLB

As the Father has loved me, so have I loved you. Now remain in my love.
John 15:9, NIV

We can rejoice, too, when we run into problems and trials, for we know that they are good for us—they help us learn to be patient. And patience develops strength of character in us and helps us trust God more each time we use it until finally our hope and faith are strong and steady.
Romans 5:3-4, TLB

And we know that God causes all things to work together for good to those who love God, to those who are called according to His purpose.
Romans 8:28, NASB

If God is for us, who can be against us?
Romans 8:31, NIV

No temptation has overtaken you but such as is common to man; and God is faithful, who will not allow you to be tempted beyond what you are able, but with the temptation will provide the way of escape also, that you may be able to endure it.
1 Corinthians 10:13, NASB

God is not a God of confusion but of peace.
1 Corinthians 14:33, RSV

Just as the sufferings of Christ flow over into our lives, so also through Christ our comfort overflows.
2 Corinthians 1:5, NIV

We do not lose heart. Though outwardly we are wasting away, yet inwardly we are being renewed day by day. For our light and momentary troubles are achieving for us an eternal glory that far outweighs them all. So we fix our eyes not on what is seen, but on what is unseen. For what is seen is temporary, but what is unseen is eternal.

2 Corinthians 4:16-18, NIV

And He said to me, "My grace is sufficient for you, for My strength is made perfect in weakness." Therefore most gladly I will rather boast in my infirmities, that the power of Christ may rest upon me. Therefore I take pleasure in infirmities, in reproaches, in needs, in persecutions, in distresses, for Christ's sake. For when I am weak, then I am strong.

2 Corinthians 12:9-10, NKJV

For we have great joy and consolation in your love, because the hearts of the

saints have been refreshed by you, brother.
Philemon 7, NKJV

There remains therefore a rest for the people of God.
Hebrews 4:9, NKJV

God . . . bound himself with an oath, so that those he promised to help would be perfectly sure and never need to wonder whether he might change his plans. He has given us both his promise and his oath, two things we can completely count on, for it is impossible for God to tell a lie.
Hebrews 6:17-18, TLB

Blessed is a man who perseveres under trial; for once he has been approved, he will receive the crown of

life, which the Lord has promised to those who love Him.
James 1:12, NASB

The effectual fervent prayer of a righteous man availeth much.
James 5:16, KJV

Let him have all your worries and cares, for he is always thinking about you and watching everything that concerns you.
1 Peter 5:7, TLB

Mercy, peace, and love be multiplied to you.
Jude 2, NKJV

A FUTURE AND A HOPE

"I've read the last page of the Bible.
It's all going to turn out all right."
Billy Graham

Know therefore that the LORD your God is God; he is the faithful God, keeping his covenant of love to a thousand generations of those who love him and keep his commands.
Deuteronomy 7:9, NIV

Don't be afraid, for the Lord will go before you and will be with you; he will not fail nor forsake you.
Deuteronomy 31:8, TLB

The Lord himself is my inheritance, my prize. He is my food and drink, my highest joy! He guards all that is mine. He sees that I am given pleasant brooks and meadows as my share! What a wonderful inheritance!
Psalm 16:5-6, TLB

Surely goodness and mercy shall follow me all the days of my life; and I

will dwell in the house of the LORD forever.
Psalm 23:6, NKJV

Behold, the eye of the LORD is on those who fear Him, on those who hope in His mercy.
Psalm 33:18, NKJV

He will never abandon his people. They will be kept safe forever.
Psalm 37:28, TLB

I will praise you forever for what you have done; in your name I will hope, for your name is good. I will praise you in the presence of your saints.
Psalm 52:9, NIV

The righteous . . . are planted in the house of the LORD, they flourish in the courts of our God. They still bring

forth fruit in old age, they are ever full
of sap and green.
Psalm 92:12-14, RSV

The LORD will fulfill his purpose for me;
your love, O LORD, endures forever.
Psalm 138:8, NIV

The path of the godly leads to life. So
why fear death?
Proverbs 12:28, TLB

The reward of humility and the fear of
the LORD are riches, honor and life.
Proverbs 22:4, NASB

He will swallow up death in victory;
and the Lord GOD will wipe away
tears from off all faces; and the rebuke
of his people shall he take away from
off all the earth: for the LORD hath
spoken it.
Isaiah 25:8, KJV

You will keep in perfect peace him whose mind is steadfast, because he trusts in you.

Isaiah 26:3, NIV

And He shall be the stability of your times, a wealth of salvation, wisdom, and knowledge.

Isaiah 33:6, NASB

Behold, I will do a new thing, now it shall spring forth; shall you not know it? I will even make a road in the wilderness and rivers in the desert.

Isaiah 43:19, NKJV

For I am offering you my deliverance; not in the distant future, but right now! I am ready to save you.

Isaiah 46:13, TLB

Your words are what sustain me; they are food to my hungry soul. They

bring joy to my sorrowing heart and
delight me.
Jeremiah 15:16, TLB

"For I know the plans I have for you,"
declares the LORD, "plans to prosper
you and not to harm you, plans to give
you hope and a future."
Jeremiah 29:11, NIV

Then maidens will dance and be glad,
young men and old as well. I will turn
their mourning into gladness; I will
give them comfort and joy instead of
sorrow.
Jeremiah 31:13, NIV

It is of the LORD's mercies that we
are not consumed, because his com-
passions fail not. They are new
every morning: great is thy faithfulness.
Lamentations 3:22-23, KJV

The LORD is good to those who wait
for Him, to the soul who seeks Him.
It is good that one should hope and
wait quietly for the salvation of the
LORD.

Lamentations 3:25-26, NKJV

For men are not cast off by the Lord
forever. Though he brings grief, he
will show compassion, so great is his
unfailing love. For he does not willingly bring affliction or grief to the
children of men.

Lamentations 3:31-33, NIV

The LORD their God will save them on
that day as the flock of his people.
They will sparkle in his land like jewels in a crown. How attractive and
beautiful they will be!

Zechariah 9:16-17, NIV

And His mercy is upon generation after generation toward those who fear Him.
Luke 1:50, NASB

If ye continue in my word, then are ye my disciples indeed; and ye shall know the truth, and the truth shall make you free.
John 8:31-32, KJV

I have come that they may have life, and have it to the full.
John 10:10, NIV

I give them eternal life, and they shall never perish.
John 10:28, NKJV

In my Father's house are many mansions: if it were not so, I would have

told you. I go to prepare a place for you.
John 14:2, KJV

In this world you will have trouble. But take heart! I have overcome the world.
John 16:33, NIV

If the Spirit of him who raised Jesus from the dead is living in you, he who raised Christ from the dead will also give life to your mortal bodies through his Spirit, who lives in you.
Romans 8:11, NIV

Overwhelming victory is ours through Christ who loved us enough to die for us.
Romans 8:37, TLB

Be joyful in hope, patient in affliction, faithful in prayer.
Romans 12:12, NIV

For whatever things were written before were written for our learning, that we through the patience and comfort of the Scriptures might have hope.
Romans 15:4, NKJV

For as in Adam all die, even so in Christ shall all be made alive. The last enemy that shall be destroyed is death. But thanks be to God, which giveth us the victory through our Lord Jesus Christ.
1 Corinthians 15:22, 26, 57, KJV

He has put his brand upon us—his mark of ownership—and given us his

Holy Spirit in our hearts as guarantee that we belong to him and as the first installment of all that he is going to give us.
2 Corinthians 1:22, TLB

Therefore, since we have such a hope, we are very bold.
2 Corinthians 3:12, NIV

Therefore, if anyone is in Christ, he is a new creation; the old has gone, the new has come!
2 Corinthians 5:17, NIV

And I am sure that God who began the good work within you will keep right on helping you grow in his grace until his task within you is finally finished on that day when Jesus Christ returns.
Philippians 1:6, TLB

Now may the Lord of peace himself give you peace at all times and in every way. The Lord be with all of you.
2 Thessalonians 3:16, NIV

Now there is in store for me the crown of righteousness, which the Lord, the righteous Judge, will award to me on that day—and not only to me, but also to all who have longed for his appearing.
2 Timothy 4:8, NIV

He . . . shared in their humanity so that by his death he might destroy him who holds the power of death—that is, the devil—and free those who all their lives were held in slavery by their fear of death.
Hebrews 2:14-15, NIV

This certain hope of being saved is a strong and trustworthy anchor for our souls, connecting us with God himself.
Hebrews 6:19, TLB

Let us hold fast the confession of our hope without wavering, for He who promised is faithful.
Hebrews 10:23, NASB

God hath given to us eternal life, and this life is in his Son. He that hath the Son hath life; and he that hath not the Son of God hath not life. These things have I written unto you that believe on the name of the Son of God; that ye may know that ye have eternal life, and that ye may believe on the name of the Son of God.
1 John 5:11-13, KJV

To him that overcometh will I give to eat of the tree of life, which is in the midst of the paradise of God.

Revelation 2:7, KJV